D1139082

Where are the
FOOTBALL LEGENDS?

Can you find the world's top footballers?

100% UNOFFICIAL

igloobooks

Where are the
FOOTBALL
LEGENDS?

Can you find the world's top footballers?

For a top footballer, life can be a game of two halves. First, there's the discipline: the fat-free, fun-free diet; the relentless fitness regime; the endless hours of training.

When you're off the pitch, however, there's the luxury lifestyle: the huge mansions; the parties; the fast cars and of course the great hairstyles.

So, what's a superstar footballer's life really like behind the scenes? Where does he go to express his true self? We've been lucky enough to secure an intimate look at some football megastars in their downtime.

You might find the likes of Neymar Jr. on the training pitch. He's certainly got a trick or two up his sleeve.

Head on over to the airport and discover who the fans are hoping to get a glimpse of. Luis Suárez, perhaps? Or Messi? Find the crowds and the guys in sharp-dressed suits on their way to another away game.

It's tough keeping in shape, so check out the salon and see who's enjoying a well-earned pampering session. David Beckham has a stylish image to maintain, after all!

No matter who you are, there's no place like home to unwind with a few mates, especially if your home is anything like Ronaldo's! Go on, see who's riding inflatable unicorns in the swimming pool.

So now it's your turn. Use your skills as a super football fan and see if you can spot all the stars, the trophies, Paul the octopus and even Pickles the dog!

Who can you spot...?

758936140 758936140

Cristiano Ronaldo

Neymar Jr.

Lionel Messi

Marcelo

Kylian Mbappé

Sergio Agüero

Luis Suárez

Gareth Bale

Paul Pogba

Eden Hazard

Harry Kane

Zlatan Ibrahimović

Luka Modrić

Sergio Ramos

Mohamed Salah

Robert Lewandowski

Giorgio Chiellini

Thomas Müller

Training Pitch

758936140
758936140

Hair Salon

758936140

758936140

Stadium

758936140
758936140

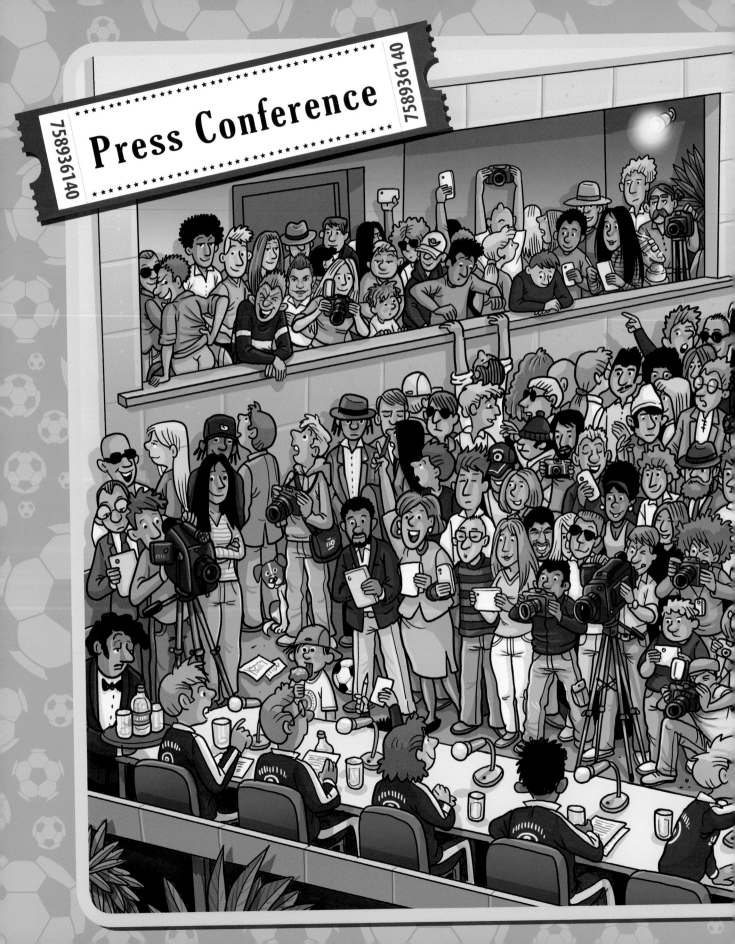

Night Clubbing

758936140

Mansion Party

758936140   758936140

Open-Top Bus Tour

758936140
758936140

Commentators' Studio

758936140

758936140

Diego Maradona –
This diminutive Argentinian striker is perhaps best known for his World Cup appearances. In 1986 he won the Golden Ball for player of the tournament.

Pelé –
Voted Player of the Century in 1999, Brazilian forward Pelé is widely regarded as the most gifted footballer of all time.

David Beckham –
This iconic English midfielder is known for his miraculous crossing and bending free kicks. He was England captain for six years.

Ronaldo –
Despite serious injuries, Ronaldo has influenced a generation of strikers. Three times FIFA World Player of the Year, he helped Brazil win two World Cups.

Zinedine Zidane –
After winning the FIFA World Cup in 1998 and the UEFA Euro 2000 with France, Zidane was awarded the Légion d'Honneur and became a national hero.

Bobby Charlton –
One of England's World Cup winners and recipient of the Ballon d'Or in 1966, Charlton was renowned for his sense of fair play.

Edgar Davids –
Once nicknamed 'the Pitbull' for his determination, this Dutch midfielder enjoyed a successful career with Europe's biggest clubs.

Paolo Maldini –
This former captain of Italy held a record number of national caps. He played his whole club career at Milan, the same club as his father.

George Best –
A fun-loving character on and off the field, this hugely talented winger helped Manchester United to their first ever European Cup.

Lothar Matthäus –
This German midfielder holds one of the finest records in the international game. He appeared in five World Cups, leading his team to victory in 1990.

Raúl –
One of Real Madrid's most important players ever, this Spanish striker was as elegant as he was prolific for both club and country.

Roberto Baggio –
This Italian midfielder had skills a-plenty and a famous ponytail. As well as his national side, he played for club teams Juventus and Fiorentina.

Hakan Şükür –
Turkey's stand-out player, nicknamed 'Bull of the Bosphorus', Şükür made his name with Galatasaray. He scored the fastest ever World Cup goal in 2002.

Carlos Valderrama –
This Colombian superstar is considered one of the best South American midfielders of all time. He was twice named South American Player of the Year.

Jari Litmanen –
Regarded as Finland's greatest player, Litmanen played for top clubs Ajax, Barcelona and Liverpool. He was Finland's captain from 1996-2008.